clash

POETRY

Cover and interior by Joel Amat Güell

joelamatguell.com

Printed in the United States of America.

ISBN: 9781955904766

Published by CLASH Books, Troy, NY.

clashbooks.com

POETRY

War
Is Not My
Mother

A Postmodern Twist for the Classic Craft

Vi Khi Nao

Contents

Acknowledgements

The poet wishes to thank the following editors and literary outlets for publishing earlier versions of these poems.

Dao Strom | *She Who Has No Masters* | "Confusion," "One Day I'll Have Vietnam Again," "Northern Mourning" & "War Is Not My Mother"

Daniel Beauregard | *OOMPH! Press* | "Ectothermic Women"

Erica Theresa Avey | *SPECTRA Poets* | "False Tanka(s)" & "Petition the Air"

Rachael Allen | *GRANTA* | "Opium," "Soak the Government in Ashes" & "Violets Grasping for Air"

Tiffany Lin | *24 VIEWS* | "Tết"

Hannah Bonner | *BRINK* | "Water Bean"

Dr. Sian Proctor | *Curated Poem Collection by Inspiration4* | "Within Ten Seconds" & "Orpheus is a Verb"

Mallory Imler Powell | *Washing Square Review* | "Jacket"

Elizabeth Metzger | *LA Review of Books* | "Water and Rice"

War
Is Not My
Mother

Confusion

The night dresses itself in ammunition
What I thought were bullets were actually stars
This was what it was like for me the second time I landed in
Saigon from the States
To the memory of the war in which I haven't been born yet.
Does the city remember my mother's childhood here?

Happiness is confusing an ambush for peace
Happiness is confusing fish sauce for beer
Happiness is confusing painkillers for ma túy
Happiness is confusing poker cards for potato chips
Happiness is confusing warmth for smoke
Happiness is confusing infinity for handcuffs
Happiness is confusing salad dressing for Julius Caesar
Happiness is confusing your aunt for a moped
Happiness is confusing PayPal for penpal
Happiness is confusing a blouse for a blanket
Happiness is confusing an enemy for an enema
Happiness is confusing a roll of toilet paper for Apple speakers
Happiness is confusing French fries for short chopsticks
Happiness is confusing amnesia for ignorance
Happiness is confusing a wedding vow for a lawn mower
Happiness is confusing cordate herbs for salmon
Happiness is confusing honey for sticky urine
Happiness is confusing lips for slippers
Happiness is confusing marriage for loneliness
Happiness is confusing menstrual pads for handkerchiefs
Happiness is confusing scissors for candies
Happiness is confusing kéo for kẹo
Happiness is confusing and (và) for mend (vá)
Happiness is confusing station (ga) for chicken (gà)
Happiness is confusing cheek (má) for ghost (ma)
Happiness is confusing scream (la) for leaf (lá)
Happiness is confusing father (ba) for madam (bà)
Happiness is confusing chant (ca) for fish (cá)
Happiness is confusing me (ta) for dozen (tá)
Happiness is confusing skin (da) for yes (dạ)
Happiness is confusing womanizer (dê) for easy (dễ)
Happiness is confusing tight (bó) for suite (bộ)
Happiness is confusing difficult (khó) for storage (kho)
Happiness is confusing a glass of water for the ocean
Happiness is confusing a man for a woman
Happiness is confusing sadness for depression
Happiness is confusing white chocolate chips for earplugs
Happiness is confusing emptiness for bait

Vinous Intentions

(for Lizard who isn't afraid of first-rate tacos)

You have tossed me into a glass of white wine
salvaged by an atomic winery
on the outer rim of California
Were you born colorless?
fueled by time
and not distance,
fermented in gravel, bitumen, sugar
detoxed for clarity.

Carafe of wasted incarnadine grapes,
near reticent cellar doors and somatic plants,
above Prince in freezing frames on a Superbowl afternoon,
now fervent radio stations and cardboard carboys.

Wine victimized by sloth and obesity.
Wine shipwrecked
by beer sewage and bacteria.
Wine sentenced to French kiss
rubber stoppers & dưỡng khí oxy
& deionized water.

Wine like the taste of reused glass
Arabic, 17th century, & deranged.
You don't know, do you?
Wine, micro-badly brewed for authentic
public consumption.

Wine for desolate poets & motorists
capsized by the Eucharist.

Wine made by dark Egyptians,
by the Mediterranean Sea,
by vinegar smelling locals.

Wine is blood, that crimson fluid
that circulates the veins & main
arteries of a city
with its empty calories & valor.

Wine is a bridge balanced between
sin
  and
    gin
      or
        heroin
          and
            distaste

a savory tang
fated for a designated
driver who has volunteered
to Uber drive Jesus to your wine-less wedding after his
three-day vacation at a resort called The Crucifixion.

Lilac & Linen

Purple sylphs,
hushed daughters kneeling in altars,
breaking bread & wine indiscreet

The autumn afternoon wrapped in moisture and rime,
like a chthonic present

These lilacs open singularly,
less rạng rỡ
than some marigolds frozen near the garden hose
whose heliotropic faces have been chastised by droplets of moonlight,
have never seen darkness,
and become silent & demented when exposed to sunlight

These florets gather light from the early mornings
wake up to other phaetons of aging
—impervious to the stillness of solar chariots—
yet their lips hunt for kisses that will only sleep diurnally;
the daughters of ephemerality desire to
gaze at their replica near a senescent well

Their breasts have been confiscated by transsexuality,
their mouths slip out of their bodies like an echo from a linen sack.

Violets Gasping For Air

To be with me or to toss me in a war zone, does it matter?
Two gallons of soymilk rear-end each other— by then the authority between us
broke
   apart newton by newton,
the cybernetic coil in the zenith— however lonely
& now you gaffe a body for a body. Near Vietnam
newsworthy mechanisms are trending: tsunami
volatile, violins and violets gasping for air,
virtual videos held captive in a vault, virgins & victims abandoned in warehouses,
Edward's pheasants chained to caves and waterfalls.
You surrender your SUVs to be near me
You cook green beans near a military base to receive one glance from me.
You rescind your gaseous words of assault against the enemy of communism
   to have me.
Somehow it doesn't matter what you do
since your blunder is that you often oversleep.
You allow a ball of fire to fall into a river. You
know nothing about the deceit of sacrifice.
You suffocate me & left me isolated in a recycling bin.

Near the bathroom tile, you surrender your collarbone

You know my voice is tense. The birds evaporate easily
unlike asking a cloud to stop moving.
In the distance the private song it sings is vaporous.
Large mountains, snowcapped, bối rối.
They stand in shock from permanent immobility.
By then heaven had locked her gates.
Below, the city opens her eyes
Can't tell if it's a cloudy day or if it's wearing sunglasses
It's a city dressed in pollution & toxins
Even the moon has to spoon a satellite to avoid
second-hand lung cancer
By the end of November—
the herons have been outnumbered by apathy.
To swim against a current we know too well:
This is no road to health
Green is not a sign of wealth. It's copper poisoning.
After a day or two, a couple hike up the alp,
to abandon their only child: a gas station.
If the sky lowers her voice? From gray to cobalt?
Can you still hear the mountain singing?

Northern Mourning

phở bò đặc biệt has the following floating ingredients:
1 broken thumb of ginger, some gashed cardamom pods

1 mini cinnamon stick to echo the remaining
leg of a việt boy shelled out by the HueyCobra
3 medium-sized white onions, mirroring the skulls of
three Việt Cộngs after a bomb explosion in a Củ Chi tunnel
6 pounds of human bones, human tendon, human shank,
human sirloin & human eye or meatballs for taste & mutilation effects

1 fresh bag of bánh phở tươi
in memory of the flesh of dead white soldiers
floating down the Mekong river

1 star anise & 6 cloves: symbols of our
courage before we exploded
lastly, 1 tablespoon of crushed peppercorn:
the ashes before the war

float all of these in a pot
simmer them for the next 63 years on a coal stove

*best served with nụ cười, thai basil, chili peppers, limes,
beansprouts, nước mắm, chopped scallions, hoisin & hot sauce

Rings Of Rebirths

Slain dreams want
To be immortals, iced
By chimerical metal, ferocious
Ambient voice, saliva-bearing

After a hallucination, our mind
Will resent the birth of an illusion
So why won't we beg the river to drown us?
How much water does it take to engulf a girl without dreams?

Chiến tranh doesn't mean less contrition
Time in the military will climb a tree
Before falling asleep by lithographing senescent rings
Of rebirths.

Inside the funeral home of our post-war desire,
Survivors discipline
Their mirth by
Escorting pomegranates into a bomb shelter

Every doornail wants to be desolate
Pounding rivets into the music of wood
The forest is not entirely ligneous
Moisture doesn't always resemble wood.

My Face In Her Dishwasher

the idiomatic language of yearning:

her collarbone keeps me awake at night, like the hooves of an equestrian bandit, racing against the muscle of the forest away from the wasteland of my desire.

in time, the body gets used to the horses of needs, as they heave and tug forward, the ropes expecting a second chance at ambushing muteness. The night before, I placed my face into her dishwasher, the next morning my eyelids are stacked against a cereal box.

i want her to show forces of sovereign law, a book spread open by a pine cone. As if she is flawless. As if she is flawless and sharp.

a bowl of moonlight falls asleep on a spoon. After the satellite of the earth leaves us, we begin to want what we can't have: even if that want is 29.5 days.

sodium hydroxide:

lather the nervous system
with enough bubbles, airtight
where thrashing is forbidden.

how to bring froth forward?
when saliva slips out of the tongue,
nebulously,
innocently,
and disquietingly

the ribbons of nudity want their photographs
of limpidity to swim against ánh sáng
while your heart plummets into skim milk
a cereal box doesn't understand the language of blinking
like two women scissoring
against a tofu mattress
your morality is naked
but not your wit
how does it feel to bathe
yourself in homosexuality?

At Mười Giờ Rưỡi, Jesus Snapchats W/ Judas

To assure
that he has forgiven him.
Suicide isn't the way to redeem oneself after betrayal,
especially since silver is certainty not worth more than eternity,
but what if your betrayal awards everyone
salvation? —
(here silver is worth more than gold because it stimulates immortality.)
Why Snapchat —

you asked Jesus?
as the primary tool of scriptural communication, when time is easily eliminated,
when Jesus holds —
the app with teeth, without chronological consent, against his pre-resurrected
face
and miraculously whispers to Judas
"On behalf of humanity —Thank you for betraying me."
Judas gazes through the peephole lens of himself
weeps tears made of silver coins
as he watches Jesus being crucified on his Android phone
biblical content — he will lose — within 24 hours
although inaccessible now
Judas did notice dấu cộng & smiley virtual stickers
disappearing & since damnation is mostly eternal —

That's why. Forgiveness is best given in a time-based medium.

Water & Rice

rice I

Each grain is one
Eye slanted towards hell,
Water me until my body
Becomes nước đá
Soaked in artificial agriculture.

water II

My impulse for her
Takes too long
To take a bath
In a washbasin
Called desire & compulsion.

rice III

Grown in Asia
To treat sprains & bruises:
Rest now ice
Before I compress
You in my own mountain

water IV

Colorless & tasteless
I want him commercial & cold,
Dressed in oxygen & hydrogen.
His viscosity is my tension,
This ion of temporality.

rice V

Wild in a swampy paddy
Thrashing with husk,
I want her flooding me
On my hillsides, in long terms
Sleeping in me like a crescent.

Haiku

Baldness is a floor;
It only squeaks your sàn nhà
If you walk on hói

Sadacre

Your face is standing near the door of my sadness,
inside a house made of nothing, pressing against the plexiglass

of the shooting range of my depression, in goggles & determination
the surround sound of the bullseye target, the bullet of

amnesia, the grenade of memory—Fall stains, ochre sorrow
and turquoise pain and then the umbrella catches the rainshower—

of melancholy. You are lost in your thoughts: I was just a door
you couldn't unlock and the clouds hover over us like tàu vũ trụ,

its aluminum façade a second mirror or lake for our hidden sky
that night I refused to make love to the five different fires of mania

or to a reticent patio sitting alone in a sphinxlike forest—
all the appliances in this vacant house are charged to a wall,

plunging ennui into the abyss of my nearly empty expression,
a depravity of modernity, & beyond it, the inevitable void,

the illusions of subsistence cleaving ethos by ethos
into a vocal cord outsung by an un-sonic veil—a fog of damnation:

it's not a polar bear crying into a pinecone, but a bush
hushed by loneliness, hallucinations, & despondency &

insulated from the turbine of pain killers & anti-depressants,
I am standing against the basin of time, near an Android phone—

a device that can't mirror the higher strata of my subconscious
an electronic ruler to post-measure history against history:

If a smart phone has to announce to the world that it is smart
It's like telling an ego that its self-image belongs to the number zero,

whose magnitudes are reduced to a disarrangement of binary codes:
she/her, their/them, he/him, she/him, he/her, their/she, it/they,

and who is right to say: gender isn't an emotional game of Tetris
a collapsing playground of incongruency, sadder than conformity?

Our psyche is walking around in an anthropogenic beauty parlor
waking up gas stations, spas & saunas, lawnmowers, nail salons by

driving a bipolar drone called being human into a polar bear
whose coat is a sad case of dandruff and thinks that hyperthermic

intraperitoneal chemotherapy is a kind of climate change or
an interactive 3-D simulator only seen in war zones.

Soak The Government In Ashes

I

After one Communist term, the cloudbursts
Become so authoritative
In their dragon of heir in-transparency
A Confucius tree walks to its first sight
Of arboreal gunfire from the north
Ca sĩ Hương Lan soaks silhouettes
With her nine-layered voice
At midnight, the clay sets out to
Unbundle its five-hundred-year-old mud
War sobs bind their soul to one ministry
Wailing for the battlefield of bribery
To become a public servant tomorrow
Tuberculous has to return to Moscow
Aubades revisit colonialism
The monsoons remain out of tune
How high up there is the yellow star of socialism?

II

A soldier weeps next to his wife
His mind hidden inside a blade
The serpent way to combat infertility
Each word is an infantryman
Marking the hoof prints of a thousand stones
The tree seeks death in one yellow rose petal
Our sabbatical days memorize war music
The plant collecting wind with its herbaceous shirt
Harmony waters its own eardrum
While the wet grass grows weary
From oblivion & fading
Two raincoats ambulate in the rain
Moisture is not a man dressed in cloth
Serenity has no servants
Without masters, war doesn't have to wait
For her to fall asleep on a stone
A postcard revisits a battlefield, Điện Biên Phủ
The monsoons have a way of listening
To the French rap songs of mortars & artilleries
For 1 month, 3 weeks, 3 days
Without having to forcefully subdue
Fireworks on their way to being wet soot.
In Vietnamese, Điện means electricity
& Phủ is a sexy military word for "shield." And,
Do you really need a literal translation or dossier
For the middle name of one battlefield?

III
Cải lương splits the throat of tradition
With her octave mourning
Lamenting is a revolutionary word
For enemy
To unfriend the refrain of sorrow
One must break the ribcage of a city
Watch it struggle to breathe
Its combat tents bruise like a pair
Of collapsed lungs
If he can't breathe, he won't sing
The injured soldier of a city
Must clutch his heart like a grenade
Above, the mountains
Have found a way to live
With independence & war crimes
Hồ Chí Minh sleeps in his grave
With one eye opened, one eye closed
Fish sauce is a kind of pelagic sodium
Not fermented by the smoke of war
Sleeping in clear cylinder glasses
Pretending to be malted beer
When torn from water, what fish doesn't conform?

Jacket

My heart is a jacket sipping tea
My leather is xấu xí, my lining a mammal
Revered queen, if you insist on putting me on you
Please stretch my taut vulva first by bending my knees

You Soak & I Cry

You ngâm and I khóc:
before the boat docks
paucity in the senses,
flora in the aura.

After the gale of summer,
yesterday, sadly, I yielded
to a tempest in a teapot which
nghẹn ngào to tears in a storm!

Your tenderness is my glove
that clothes mùa đông in my
heart & forces the lieutenant
of frost to quickly depart.

By fleeing, I close more doors
than suicidal jellyfish arriving on
đường bờ, I can't rivet
what hasn't been unfastened.

Ah, please don't iron my bao tay
when stain shows so much
disdain for my hands when
there is so much tội lỗi to gain!

On behalf of that anti-task, by
pure compulsory revulsion,
you deplore the discoloration
of that glove I once dyed for you.

Ôi, don't wear or swear
the earth is no closet for reflection
impersonating only to smear
the garment of rejection.

To leak love inconspicuously
by your sweat glances, I forebear
I will never need you for
anything more than winter.

The Church And Its Pale Betel Leaves

It's late summer, on
a Philippine hill— the church and pale leaves—
While the sea-torn Vietnamese
refugees climb this đỉnh núi to clutch their daily refuge
as priests impaling prayers on their palms
Below, a sea of makeshift tents
Test the breeze by lifting her skirts
One Việt crone has transfixed her war-torn sight
on the young stove she has just fostered
from splinters and stones found on the island's ridge
The heavy rain guns down this refugee city, like ammunition,
impaling the immodest tents
& battering the stopgap stove until dust and debris remain
The tortured woman wails
When it gets dark again & the storm
revisits the graveyard of its destruction
The lights high up on the ylang-ylang trees
weep with wet moth-embodied tears
The air is gray,
quivering at each senescent lament
The bánh bao shaped clouds even take out their stratospheric hands
Shaking each other while billowing,
"Peace be with you. Peace be with you."
The storm reminds Mary of her chaos of influence
The bánh bèo molded moon
squirrels away her rice flour
When the air is clean again
The refugees come out of their hiding
and study the wreckage
made from the phở bò of the storm— broth dark & damp with too much battered
cilantro
Three cloves walk to the broken water pump, holding each other's hands
Survival is a slaughterhouse!
The scrawny feet of the Vietnamese
skulk around the wasteland of their homelessness—
At the đồi gió hú of their misery,
the refugees rebuild their debris
Months later
When it is time to serve the bone-thin broth—fresh mint, basil, parsley chase after
the tongue like giggling girls, sedated by the hidden fragrance of black pepper,
scallion, ginger
The refugees are the ylang-ylang trees
yellowed & scented by poverty & adversity
They re-stitch the widening holes of their nets
They refuse to give hospitality to mosquitos
Even a slaughterhouse is a house

Hindquarter cuts are still a deluxe
Brisket, flank steak, chuck roast
still can make the broth sweet & juicy
The Vietnamese don't need the most expensive cuts to make their broth—
An empty
aluminum bucket revisits
the water pump
that the storm wrecked
When the cloves
walk the rainwater
home & pour
it into the pot sitting firmly
on three stones
The calamity-battered crone
flashes forth her crowfeet by emptying her widest smile
Later when her lips leak blood
We know it is not from pain
It's leisure behaving like
chewed betel leaf

Hello Gothenburgers

I am Leila Ali Elmi, the newest member of your Swedish
Parliament in hijab & for my Vietnamese people who
are segregated at the coastline of immobility
My imminent term in office is decisive
& unaided & celebrated by the engine of
your intransient, immigrant voice
I, who love the exit signs
of ghettoization, criminality, illegibility,
have found stability in instability
as I seek to un-employ
your Somalian isolation &
deprivation
My mouth will become your
bread and my voice
will become your clean water;

My dear beloved 370,000
asylum seekers & immigrants
I intend on bending the formality
of our malnourished education
with uninvited literacy
Our ignorance won't be grassrooted
in the back court of Swedish cordiality
Nothing can hush
our future constructed schools
from ethnic fertility.

After you bathe your racial
legs in this socioeconomical lake
ready or not,
I am prepared to tackle overcrowding
by overcrowding our parliament
with my education reforms
After you whiten your white teeth
with coconut flesh or lighten your flesh
with Otaheite gooseeberry (chùm ruột)
I invite you to alter our routine dinner
menu of Molotov cocktails & plate
of grenades with a banquet
of tables & chairs & pen & pencil
Books will be our appetizers
Effective teachers as our main course
I am not just & only your
liberal Muslim in this suburb
I am your universal interpreter
& interlocutor for your inequality

As you already know,
nothing can be done alone
help me help you help us.

Lesbian Snowflakes

1
Freeze the lake, Người Phụ Nữ Đồng Tính Luyến Ái, from its opulent air.

2
Feathery ice mistresses:
won't your memory of us
retreat?

3
At once, bring me
your beauty
one crystal at a time

4
The lake rip(ple)s out her mirror
Tastes amnesia as ice

5
"She is running away, Mỵ Nương;
classy Công Chúa is running.
How shall we isolate her?"

"Thaw your snowflakes, senescent kings.
And wear my nightcaps
inside your briefs."

6
No, sit still for Snow White!

7
Bow now, seven sư phụ giả,
The ice spear is here.

8
The spoon is asleep. And the Pillow wide awake.
        In the morning light.
                Years [thời gian] leave behind
A few concubines.

9
You foresee the degree.
Only a sperm
bank distinguishes
seed from oil

10
You rewire
And I haze.

11
Just in case, I am rice.

12
A dove
can be my fire
Công Chúa ơi...

13
      Snow
A winter blanket...

14
      Snow
florals falling
on the shoulders
of tall pine trees.

15
So same-sex snowflakes solidify your
impulse,
willpower,
a howling symmetry.

16
Like a cake
wrapped in icing,
A snowflake pulls me into her arms.

17
It was love at first sight, Ether,
Especially after a night spent
in an ice chamber without hex or sex.

America Don't Envy Us

Our life is urine & feces filled   with salty   memory of our family of 6 in
a boat   pruned hands & vomited   bodies   rocking back & forth to the
nursery rhyme of the sea 3 days   3 nights the perimeter   of the unknown
the clumsy darkness of   Our boat a thalassic coffin concealing 30 of us from
raping pirates   cá mập   drowning   after 72 hours of chthonic fright &
distress the waves   dumped   us towards   đảo Pulau Bidong   I clutched
clumps of   Malaysian sand &   poured it onto my lice-infused   head & self
anointed myself at age 9 as the new

                         princess of   refuge: It is   easy to escape Vietnam: all
we need to do is: abandon   all our extended family (aunts, cousins,
grandmothers, uncles, etc) & friends   sell all our sewing machines   & our
house & everything off our back   face indefinite   prison time if we fail to make
it (which we have) & face shame   torture   & starvation & empty-handedness
(which we have)/   When we arrive in America   instead   of streets paved w/
gold, my father worked as a corn detasseler and later as a   manual laborer in
a car factory for   nearly 30 years while my mother also worked there   while
juggling two jobs carrying heavy trays of food twice her size for a university &
later everyone discovers that I am a lesbian too

America don't envy us
We bleed a lot not just from
That war but from being near you

Opium

For Trưng Trắc (徵側) and Trưng Nhị (徵貳) (1750—1848)
The two most famous matriarchal leaders of Vietnam

My mother has a way of taking
her pain out on my brother by beating
him to a pulp with a sugarcane

my father   'hid behind
the curtain of rain, mung beans,
hủ tiếu steams, ginseng, immobility'

when it was time for my brother
to hate

he chose my father
his bystander over his abuser,
my mother, for the
inevitable scars tucked

Beneath the manhood of his adolescent thighs
his calves, his unescapable addiction to
gambling, especially in the enigmatic
apertures   of   his winning, losing

A casino,

     'is an opium den for the madhouse of the psychosis'
     A place where you win by losing & lose by losing

          slot machines aren't the only ones who are a BITCH

each whim of instinct informs

me that my brother
is selective & smart at how

     He dispenses his fondness for the way
     'my father turned a blind eye against my mother's cruelty'
I was ten or twelve years old
and like my father, I was also a bystander, an abuser

that guilt that won't retreat back
into amnesia for me ever

I live beneath the heartbeat of this crime
like peeling an onion to reveal a bruise

The guilt & regret compulsion
still stays with me since

I was thirteen   I tried to

Discipline   my brother by striking his calf
with my mother's   sugarcane. It was the only
time I ever hit him and the   untranslatable
offense remains. One day at a casino in   Florida,
my brother pre-applied three to four credit   cards under
my   father's name and maxed them all out. Within
a year, my father's   credit score went from 850 to 300.
I thought my   father had it easy. My well-timed retribution:
After I struck my brother's   eleven year old leg, creating
a ribbon of   agony & sorrow the size of a bookmark
he stared   at me and with the cane still   leaning against
my hip, I stared   back at him, both in disbelief & surprise,
for a very long time. The disciplinary gaze my brother
fearlessly gave me that   afternoon was made of pity, not
hatred, not resentment. Nearly thirty years later, sitting next
to him while he drove me to the post office.   I viewed his
gaze as the first hug he ever gave me for not   knowing
any   better   or his gaze was an indefinite response to shock:
his inability to   comprehend how his sister could hurt him so

Recklessly

A river walks a
cantaloupe home
from school while
berating a monsoon
for climbing a tree.

      *

đã
    đá
        đà.

Have they already
rocked the momentum?

      *

Diacritical marks

taste themselves
          on
the stairs

of the tongue while
feeling recklessly young.

Orpheus Is A Verb

The mind, making room for Satan, lies awake   Sedates
the seatbelts of all thunderstorms, without rain, absorbs & escorts the night into —
oblivion.

Before dawn, you walk away from sin, from us. Our bucket
full of mắm tôm, you walk ahead, our dreams

drank a sip of gin, without ice,
by the time you came back from pain, I was

coaching snow how to be holy water,
while feeding horse tranquilizers to your Siamese cats.

I was also playing a harpsichord for Eurydice, from
memory & from Google chrome. You just want me, purely, to

be a desolate tree, bearing no fruits, no memory. It's
cruel to witness barrenness wearing a Wedding Ring.

Being wedded to infertility is like inhaling
carbon monoxide for the Sylvia Plath of our time. We live

for a viper pulled from a well & for tenderness.
For love? Not possible.   Well —

Orpheus is a verb.
            Even when spoken in purgatory

To disappear galaxies away because your wife
is not an apparition sucked in by the blackhole of eagerness

We could relate to Orpheus for his impatience to see her — But not
the way he sent her back to hell — & if this isn't autoerotic asphyxiation

I don't know what is.
We want the underworld to be a song
that can't be echoed back to earth
& for that glamorous face next to the torch

Light is colossal & cruel

& so is Orpheus's love for Eurydice.

Within Ten Seconds

Death gets up. Late in the afternoon. To wear a dress
that Spring has discarded inside a mirror. A willow
tree rocks her soul to sleep.
Winter sits on a melting iceberg. Washing his clothes.
His white blouse has buttons
made from the eyes of four pre-extinct polar bears.
Summer arrives wearing
a sleeveless shirt.
While unbuttoning
its skull, a leaf
takes a deep Fall breath
and has a terrible stomachache.
Sometimes the wife is compelled to slap
her husband inside their SUV. Trong vòng mười giây,
a city burns itself by falling asleep. When it wakes up, it faces
a high population of therapists. Meanwhile Lucifer
takes out a knife to scare a Lamborghini. Which is a fancy
way of saying that a river has fallen asleep at the wheel,
& as a result, two canoes crash. Into
each other and die. On the freeway of Sông Thu Bồn. If you
had to throw your head back. To see what. The dress
looks like, it will tell you:
Gần mực thì đen, gần đèn thì rạng.

Proverbs Of Violence

Fugue of loneliness has
visible properties. For a post-war mother

mending a porcelain bowl of rice with glue
from her underfed saliva

the probability of her swaying
to the amnesia of fullness is

small & duty-bound by the aftermath
of bomb shelters. Our moths

stand in front of the graveyard of
light with shards of wings

clinging to amplifiers—sound is
a virgin homegrown by the

the terrorists of opportunities,
an incendiary device

to depict hatred for the unknown.
Not desperation. As long as

there is still war
children will enlist out of misguided

proverbs of violence: mưu sự tại nhân,
thành sự tại thiên. Bombs should not leave

their intestines near a gurney, should not seek
backpacks as places of sacred shelter, waiting for

divine signals of detonation. In the future
we will see milk as opaque

fat & protein, its intellectual properties
are genetically manipulated hormones:

starvation, mastitis,
pre-made organ donations. Children

carrying guns/ pointing them at
their own mothers is not

a pre-existing condition of
climate change, climax, or greed

How liable are we of
loving a — stranger?

Must we be a
naked vial sitting barren

in the wind without memory, DNA, or
antibiotics? Post-war mothers

distinguish their tears & scars
by becoming lotus

flowers that could be
folded into medical helicopters

or sexual positions, thus fulfilling
the prophecy of cross-pollination.

False Tanka(s)

JULY

Inside its heartbeat
A small child sleeps;
Only summer
But snow still hibernates with a plow

A SEED

Death travels lightly in daylight
Forming a regiment wrecked by the sun;
Inside the soil, gingerly
A seed unfucks its luck.

JANUARY SUN

Outside the facade of wind
A barren heart wakes up its dream,
Sleepwalking
Is for limbs without photosynthesis.

SHADOW

We want to conflate
The impossible:
My alter ego travels
Far & wide without tên tôi.

Water Bean

thủy đậu is not   a bean or a bird

it's chicken pox highly contagious   when eaten with rotten pitaya

you can split the world open by creating   brand name purses & facts & twitter
fake   accounts

i am just a boy who has just   broken the law of longing

& he is thick / yes / how he came to   me on a blue lawn chair / his manhood

he fills / my appetite with meningitis

a small binary family of / sapodillas

men who have spinal

which means he loves

deterioration w/

discord with drowsiness

according to google

bright lights/

water or fake

thủy means

bean like seed of formality as in landing

news & đậu means

Ectothermic Women

I have decided to forgo my interesting life by investigating the origin of the universe, its intramural arrangements and apparatuses. I am particularly interested in where women were made and why God manufactured them since men are just fine being alone or engaging in a fancy homosexual condition called self-love. The universe was born seventeen years ago. After acing my exams in theology, I've concluded that women in our ecosystem remain intricately connected to amphibians. They are ectothermic, meaning that they rely on men for warmth, the way frogs and salamanders seek coziness on reheated rocks. However, if we annihilate the female population entirely, the way we've treated women since the beginning of time, we could save men from being inconvenient portable furnaces for women; and our ecosystem would last longer because our solar panels or "natural" masculine resources (men) wouldn't be poorly allocated or invested in love for ectothermic outlets (women). While the earth is distraught and agitated with the hyperactivity of materialistic culture and its evangelical companies, where codes of invention and commodity are deeply embedded in unrecyclable things such as sperm, polypropylene, diapers, aerosol cans, dust, medical waste, wire hangers, botox, and yogurt cups—my appetite is still propelled by the farcicality and incongruity of desire and its logic, nhỏ nhoi or supersize, Amazon or mom & pop, that shape the nonexistent vacation days of my consumption. As a telemarketer for God, I constantly make robocalls to quarantined bà già of the universe—hoaxing, swindling, feasting on their retirement and savings, obliterating their portable urine bags—and hoisting them in Amazon boxes, fastidiously pre-packaging them so that farmers in India could water their soil for the next episode of soybeans, tomatoes, sugar beets on agricultural Netflix. All in all, my useless work tests the automatonic rage or exogenic zone between quadriplegic swimmers and runners, rice and bread, miso soup and chowder. I tend to endanger education with my unorthodox research and make women's lives harder, but I think it's more important to make things worse than to make things better. I like to believe that God put me on earth so that I can retaliate against women for no apparent reason. I simply just want to be a part of God's telemarketing ploy.

Việt Particles War-Arranged On Sea Marine

inscribed to my aunt *Nguyễn Thị Hằng Huê*

one day i will put on a nón lá
in iowa for you when the first frost
of winter has taken over and my heart is a floorboard
your bony feet in plastic sandals speak their proverbs
while the midwest cold
emaciates my memories of you
some of your reveries bend their weak knees
shaking like planks
on their way home to me
be mute, loverboy

my father climbed xe đò every
month
from long khánh to miền tây
he descended the wet streets
with my mother's warm fabrics
pressed to his chest
as tailors added eyes and
buttons and costumed embroideries
to pink and green blouses
measured and made and sewn together by
my mother
late into yesterday's kerosene embodied night

at one point my mother stood
inside the prison's metal doors
still deeply pregnant with my little brother
the little village of time
opened her eyes
to witness dishonesty
the communists locked her in there overnight
to see if sewing needles and
bribery shared the same
family of stitch
incarcerated, my mother made an
official complaint
that could not be unheard

the clothes of our soul have been altered by the
sewing machine of communism
each day in the states
we bash our souls
against the stone of democracy
this is how we wash our clothes
then we hang them on
winter's clothesline, hard

and frozen like
fugitive-fed tilapias
the whites asked

why are we still so cold
despite being so bundled
they don't know we

wear ice from our necks down
to forget that we are still
very much refrigerated refugees

despite ordering burgers & fries
at mcdonald's drive thru
the ocean has a way
of pushing particles of us
in a sea flask where we could break apart
it's no doubt that war is not
my mother
my amnesia
my homeland
my bánh bèo
my burial ground
my cornfield

tell god that
WAR IS NOT MY MOTHER

tell god that
WAR IS NOT MY MOTHER

tell god that
WAR IS NOT MY MOTHER
but a
garment
made
by
death
& suffering
& speed &

fiscal msg

Sổ Mũi

In 1986 my aunt took me to an ear, nose, & throat doctor in Sài Gòn;
my nose won't cease falling liquid mucus & baby Long Khánh couldn't do anything
for me.

We passed a vast meadow of rice into Sài Gòn, a post-war metropolis whose
wrecked body
ends with a verbal noise like gone, the ringing cry of false or used—sai inside Sài
Gòn.

Three years later we got on a boat to Iowa, obeyed the identical course as the
Syrians, the boat splitting the Pacific in halves with its bow, farewell then to chợ
đêm Vũng Tàu.

32 years before I was born, the death of politician Lyuh Woon-hyung was
eloquently mourned.
A Korean rarity, like blood is not thicker than mucus, he was loved by both North
and South

The day I came into the world, two oil-tankers barreled into each other in the
Caribbean Sea
pouring 280,000 tons of crude oil on the head of Tobago like a beggar king.

After my 36th birthday, my aunt asked, Is this the year you return to Vietnam?—dì
nhớ cháu nhiều lắm. Unlike summer, the coffee beans are still hibernating.

Perhaps one day I will become a Vietnamese rarity—adored by the North of
experimentalism and the South of mainstream & able to say "hello" to my aunt in
person.

My Rapist Forgives My Mother For Getting In The Way Of Raping Me

My mom elbows her way
                        downstream.
She prioritizes.
                I rewind.
She patrols & I pigeonhole. Unfriend
fake boobs from my Facebook,
constantly bursting here,
constantly invading my Amazon
prime. She invades —I cake &
snowflake. Each year after the rape,
she revisits the graveyard of violence.
She takes out her unique binoculars
& examines the façade of sexual assault—from afar.
I cry. While my mom sucks her thumb-
nails from my iPhone. Her eyes, wet bags
of sand, full, an avalanche of revenge.
My rapist, a sadist with
a terrible credit score. He shoved
my mom four times against our unlocked door.
During his rape of me, he asked Alexa:
what is the temperature of Austin, Texas?
Afterwards my mother wailed & tailgated
my rapist in her fake Sam Edelman Patti high heels.
Alexa, play "The Power of Love." Now.
He emphasizes "NOW."
My mother resists. Làm ơn! She won't
Give up. On Celine Dion.
Or homemade Dijon mustard. On me.
After raping me, he got up to put the dishes
away from our dishwasher and wiped down
some muffin crumbs off our kitchen counter with
a few clean sheets of the Brawny paper towels,
his blood-saturated dick still hung out of his drawer
like a mangled hand sticking out of a
Chick-fil-A drive thru window.
My mom hisses. I wake up the sofa. I dine after I sin
I take after Zhang Xin.
I take after Zhang Xin. I take
after Zhang Xin paragliding down SOHO.
My mom erases her memory of the rape
with Windex—it's a glass cleaner
more powerful than club soda. Just noise &
an afternoon of fabric wing—lightweight,
recreational. Of course, the rapist liked a
clean kitchen & forks and spoons
lying faced down, pre-cleaned just like me.

Every now & then, my mom has a low
tolerance for an off-key Marie Claudette
& forgiveness.

Dear Photograph,

I am ridiculed by you after some time spent—in the mendacious hearts,
from the mendacious human clays, and on one occasion beneath an underpass
with my iPhone immovable in a pond of dehydrated giò lụa peeling sap
from a foreigner's cheekbone. This evening you were sugarcane
and bus 45. I have been startled by you, placed in a coffin by you.
Had you deliver me cà phê đá in my desired wineglass with condensed milk
and just adequate darkness. A laidback oblation. A liability of desire.
My hypnotist imparted: Periodically, it's easier to be a clay holder than it is
to be worshipped. I agreed with them since I am better at withholding
than I am at shielding. I have sexted lovers whose chest hair deterioration
I haven't erased from my consciousness. And, what about God's plans
for their baldness? It's not that I haven't shared a bladder with them.
Shouldn't I have attempted to botox my way out of desire and build a hotel
for việt kiều, or sharpened my eyebrows or shadowed Kim Kardashian
on her Kanye West detour? I wonder why Republican women love
Kavanot so much, my hypnotist observed. Politics is irreconcilable.
A supreme court nominee I briefly texted with kidnapped me. At the height
of my romantic infancy, I fell in love with him. Afterward I told myself:
I am only a sword swallower to the one who has been specifically
ordained by our Lord. I knew religion would change everything.
I decided to stare at people's collar bones when I engaged with strangers.
I yearn to smooth their wrinkled blouse with my itchy fingers, the tenderness
for my kind spinning into fable and compulsion. This small world.
I craved to touch the helper grasping my khoai môn with such raw quietness.
To hold the boy sitting across from me in a bánh cuốn stall with YouTube
in his skull and cherimoya and guava in each of his armpits. Hug
the child clinging to an oversized basket, declaring: Forget yesterday.
Her hug so small and diminishing and not designed for me.
You're too desperate, my hypnotist confronts me. No one has ever been able
to dismantle their shadow. But I believe it's good to be fraught with hopelessness.
I have urine between my first and second toes that refuses to be wiped. There is a
lamb limping in my heart. There are kidney stones waiting to leak their way out of
me. God, there are ribbons inside me that beg to be unraveled. I watched all the
TV shows on Netflix about murders and crimes and demanded that my mother-
in-law love my phở bò I want my chair pushed across a room. I tried to deny
every opportunity for you to insert a glove inside of me. But, in your handsome
aftershave, you unlock my bones with sediment and residue. By making me
stand over the sink naked and overdue, I have relinquished all of my tablets and
bonnets over to you. I sobbed beneath a rubber tree, followed your farts around
Twitter, and gave you the last straw of my toothpick for your teeth. I even forgot
Sài Gòn for you, but now I am throwing myself off this helicopter. Forget that
you were once, in 1975, a drop of dew on my lips. Forget that it's no longer the
monsoon season for misguided arrows and panty hoses. Mostly, I want your heart
to become a water buffalo and make rain clog the rice field so that I would forget
ever knowing you.

Photograph Of The Fermented Tongue In Capsule Motel With Serrated Rasceta

in Cà Mau I swallow the snake venom   Streetside Beer
sake   in Phan Thiết I grew a beard   now I feel sorry for
every kiss I ever   mislaid   now elegant   chewed betel leaves
and grapefruit rinds   this sweating   a tongueful
of acidity   as a girl I shoplifted a magenta silicone dildo
from a local pornshack near the sea   I walked back to
the apartment with it in my pocket.   &
when my foster family closed their eyes   I boiled it with water and oxtail
bones from the well and added star anise, fish sauce, cinnamon, ginger
found in a phở package   the broth bloomed
in my mouth like a scandalous water spinach   my heart unraveled
and broke open all over their cement floor   the rice noodles slithered
down my pipe   like white eels   while   a   salmon tree submits
its kimono to a king   near a Xuân Hương lake in Đà Lạt I tried to
commit suicide with a homeless girl wearing a yellow   áo bà ba
when the village fished us out of the lake, a Thai sex trafficker
asked her if she would like to be a child prostitute and she said yes
to Huế first   This changed her life but   not mine
This   does not diminish my love for her despite the fact that
they didn't offer   the same of opportunity of a lifetime to me
From time to time,   whenever I eviscerate a fish   in memory
of our   brief suicidal encounter   I remember her hair
falling like black waterfalls and I grieve   that I loved her
more than she   ever loved me   I always expected
that the next time   I chose to close my life not with a closetful
of water but with a bullet to my heart   she would stop fake-moaning
in between bedsheets and   without knowing why
drop a tear or two   for me   When she resumes   her fornication again,
I will beg her   to ask her white old men if they
like fucking her drunk and if she prefers dildos in her phở
or   pineapple cores   instead
I like to clean everything with anise seeds &   sometimes
cardamom   because sex is phở &   phở is love

Bipartisan Monarch

Notwithstanding the evening's somber monolith of downpour,
we deliver ourselves to Bùi Thị Xuân at past midnight.,
our watches still engorged with dawn. I insist,
Time insists on falling asleep and a teacher and New York man
threatened to kill supreme court nominating senators. But,
people have to get imprisoned first and things have to get
worse before things can continue to descend into hell again.
I know it's not natural to want bullets of impossibilities as
justice wades through weeds to become weed.
Our asphalt still cracked under the pressure of
ignorance. I'm angry and forlorn. I don't have institution
of being anymore and for eleven days in a row now, my lover
wakes me up to show me his cage, a tube made of electricity.
He wraps me in a leopard jacket as we confront
the political cloudburst from Lindsey Graham to Taylor Swift,
and when the abyss arrived inside the showboats, I foresaw
the unbearable future. A few millions substantially, Dr. Ford's
testimony, then Matt Damon's, and then scratchpads,
umbrella-hidden owls arrive to witness this Yale farm-raised
donkey with his ferocious beer face to finish off the virtually 36-year
American Rape Association silent revolt. A woman neighboring us,
some Pro-Trump heavyweight, knocks off a catalogue of objections
as to why this judge—this beer-loaded thoroughbred, power
and influence, so on and so forth—should conquer
this backbreaking three-month unhistorical antagonism.
Then, this mare named Susan Collins emerges,
just insouciantly galloping with her chief stallion,
and ensuing a short, deceived interruption in the rainstorm,
she's charging forth and the FBI, the fake stopper of time,
preposterously quick and deliberate so that the Democrats can
grasp fully that stonewashed astronomical blaze on injustice's
forehead like America is delusionally great again. As the elephant
reduces its temporary turmoil and we all shut our mouths to spit,
the heavyweight uncrosses her legs, and declares forcefully:
Trump is back. Because he was never gone.

Threshold

for Giovan

The day I strolled along Nguyễn Thị Minh Khai,
it was in late September and I noticed a campfire
on the torso of my blue blouse, and another on
the stomach—I think I am that gorgeous. There was an
entire era in the second millennium when it was devastating
to have campfires in your tops and quần tây.
But now it is 2018 and I chase after that fashion
statement like a dork. There was an absolute tradition of
sensationalizing your body that was more Vietnamese
than Syrian, except it was Syrian in
2010 while it was striking to be a resilient
ravenous refugee who held so little
of her own measurement and she was a fragment
of a crusade as trivial as antiquity and it floodlit the
camp fire in her blouse. It's the inauguration
of winter today, and each period has
fissures and flaws through which summer
or spring are forced to trickle out. The least
impeccable tang of it, weirdly in January. Oh recall
once I was a refugee. I seized a white
glob of bánh bao and stood up from the pond of dumplings
near my kneecaps and while bursting from the
carnal seams I marched towards
your body where there was unceasing
Bia Hanoi. By then we were drowning down
333, an ugly inferno of a drink. Near the
threshold I confided that I came for the both
of you because you were too delicious to miss.
It was evitable that the children were asleep. It's
impossible to know if I wanted bánh ít trần or donut
as it appeared that roundness was
the influential defiance thing, me feeling
inadequate about everything that wasn't round.
I was a segment of an ethos of drunks who glugged
in shacks near Lý Tự Trọng street and slurped down
the cruel Saigon beer and the sake on tap and
hallucinated about driving you around in a scooter.
Those conical parasols. I hug beer bottles wherever I go so
I can spit haikus of you in them. I must have you.
You who "đậm đà hương vị Miền Tây."
There was food in everything I owned.
I also owned two opium dens. I absolutely adored you.
Somehow it was never enough, the beginning of
my nuisance, a resurgence in my
nightmares and hallucinations which my bà nội
was afraid to impart. I was a predictable home to inmates

of dementia and sake. Though I must say:
they behaved more like mistresses than convicts.
The virtue of that night is that I didn't stop blinking once.
It was the only thingamajig that transpired
in Sài Gòn. I locked my cunt in a brothel
to block everything else out.
Like my tits were not codependent enough.
I don't feel sorry for what I did, even though
the entire world hated me.
The entire world can eat bún thịt nướng &
I won't give a fuck. I had a campfire
near the back of my purple turtleneck.
It was impossible to stop it from
sweltering. It grew bigger
and bigger. I got used to barbequing
thịt gà with lemongrass on a skewer with it.
In the 2nd week of February, it was impossible to leave
my blue hammock. My body
jolted awake at ungodly hours
and there was pháo bông
and Tết Nguyên Đán and I kept
on smoking, throwing up, and kissing the cheeks
of tea cups left and right. I couldn't forget
the second you put a red envelop
on my palm. It was like your heart
on an ashtray. I grew fond of your
doorknobs and even fucked them a couple of times
lamentably, not afraid to tell Adam
where his Adam apple is. Or how to miss a mark.
Though I was told just now I have missed the mark.
I have so many camp fires in my closet. From
all the people and memories
I haven't been able to barbeque.
I eat one plate of logic and knowledge
after another and làm gái
and a newer version of the iPhone seem to
be what people are into. Or care to share with me.
But I don't dare forget the manner in which
campfires visit my body like an
asteroid seeking for the very first
time its home
on a planet called my torso.

Synthetic

In your protracted visit, you authorize my
wastage of plastic, envisaging
robust revenue in death and suffocation. I insist
the victory in my task, chiefly
concerning sea turtles.
If I may say so boldly: I am ready
to be the sole custodian of seahorses.
Now, nếu tôi là ai, you could restrain
the solemn polyethylene, the taciturn carbon atoms that visit
me so frequently here, whereas new cities get
twenty months of organic substance abuse. You are
my only master: meanwhile,
I give nylons new heart transplants, I become an
inert digestive system for seals and sea lions
like dying is an art, and so millions of
marine birds fragmented by latex, can genuflect
with plastic debris. I forget
you are artificial, in our transitory tolerance of
that tenancy. You who prefer
man-made pollution over the ecosystem,
who think, in sequence,
exempt from procreation, as if life cannot
be shorter already, the mottled juniper,
the rushed verdures of the bonsai deteriorating
even in January, in clumsy dimness: I am the mother
of these sea bruises.

How Is It Possible That Boat People Know How To Write Poetry In English?

dear Nguyễn Du, beneath your skull how is it possible,
born in wealth, like Elizabeth Bishop, that you were able to know so much about
female
prostitution? beneath your penmanship you are also Tố Như & Thanh Hiên,
by the age of 13, you are an orphan however chrysanthemum
& you are not a leaf itself but a shrub composed of some trifling florets
at its tiara & believe me when I tell you that you wrote
your ambitious masterpiece, *The Tale of Kiều* while taking Ponstan
three times a day with bún bò huế in your liver
beneath you, but not under you, you are not an elite saffron crocus
that was born yesterday and tomorrow is a wailing game
I desire to revisit Nghi Xuân once more time to exercise
my memory which keeps crying at night like a sea-torn flower
with lotus tea by my bedside, I keep on waking up
weather-bound by your poetic sins, Nguyễn Du Nguyễn Du

The Seven Halibut Huts

Although it is a dreadfully late afternoon,
below the 2nd deck of the sailboat,
a young woman stands weaving,
her nón lá, in the near dusk virtually imperceptible,
a dusky hay-beige,
and her gaze threadbare and refined.
The sea wafts so airworn of halibuts
it forces our eyebrows to narrow.
The seven halibut huts have sharply gaunt tiles
and slender, bamboo slats sloping
to the sea markets
for several bà gánh bánh tráng to pass to and fro.
All is gold: the opaque flatness of the ocean,
engorging soporifically as if supplicant to sink under,
is milky, but the gold of the bamboo chairs,
the thùng tàu hủ nóng, and pylons, strewn
midst the desolate debris,
is of a deceptive luminosity
like the negligible timeworn shacks with a gilded toss
rising on their seaward partitions.
The halibut barrels are wholly coated
with sheets of gorgeous briny scales
and the đòn gánh share equal varnish
with buttery patinas of silver,
with colossal scintillating microbes swarming on them.
Up on the squally incline beneath the huts,
fixed in the bare buoyant splash of meadow,
is a primordial stilted spindle,
fractured, with ten drawn-out blanched levers
and some disconsolate streaks, like emaciated phlegm,
where dew and mucus have invaded.
The young woman takes a sliver of dried squid.
She was a mistress of my mother.
We chatter of the population decay
and of halibut and catfish
while she listens for a gondola to return.
There are butterfly needleworks on her blouse and on her neck.
She has bartered her body for food
from countless suitors with that sextorn body of hers,
the core of which is nearly frayed away.

Below the sea's lip,
where they drag up the liners, above the lengthy incline
sloping into the sea, bony gold
bamboo stalks are rested flat
past the ashen pebbles, muted and muted

at interludes of six or seven meters.

Icy black abysmal and unequivocally sharp,
dynamic sufferable to no human,
to land creatures and to sea turtles . . . One sea turtle specifically
I observed nightfall following nightfall.
She was fascinated by me. She was fretful about music;
like everyone with a heart, a martyr in absolute absorption,
nevertheless I used to croon her nhạc vàng trước 75.
I even chanted "Một Mai Giã Từ Vũ Khí."
She crawled out of the sea depth and studied my throat
gradually, shifting her rigid structure a bit.
Then she would dissolve her appearance, then swiftly materialize
neatly in the unchanged spot, with a nonchalant disdain
as if it there was more to life than this feeble magic
Icy black abysmal and unequivocally sharp,
the vibrant ashen arctic sea . . . Back, near us,
the exalted soaring grenades commence.
Grayish, coupling with their doom,
a billion war bullets froze inside the threshold of the sky
resting for war. The sea appears poised
above the elegiac grim and cobalt-charcoal rocks.
I met the identical sea, the identical,
slightly, inelegant horror above the pebbles,
frostily liberated beyond the rocks,
beyond the human bones and afterward the ecosphere.
If you could bathe your eyesight in destruction,
your heart would adjourn in a coma a thousand years later,
your memories would turn to bomb clouds and your eyes would become cobalt
as if annihilation were a mutation of desire
that breastfeeds on evaporating estuaries and thrives in darkness.
If you savored it, it would appear hostile,
then brackish, then indubitably scald your consciousness.
It is like what we fancy humanity to be:
murky, salty, watertight, pitiful, absolutely powerless,
fraught with the callous piercing voice
of creation, originated from the shaky depression of change
evermore, sinuous and careworn, and since
humanity is antithetical, curving always towards the unknown known.

Before The Storm

How will I unknot lightning? Before the storm?
When she squeezes into fate's wallet, altered before the storm.

"Mì quảng phú chiêm / sedating in a closet"—"Where have you been?"
God!—"what were we / when the idiom sang" before the storm?

Before we were born—Life is ungrateful!—God had to throw us into a fishbowl.
What is more as we become closer to the closet, we abate before the storm.

Delirium had us. How devastating? God's servants tearing a golden goose into
halves.
For opium, my darling, have you been poor—ever?—before the storm.

For those guava-fashioned ballerinas, I must admit:
Detain the yakult from the Minoru Shirota, before the storm.

What gave you away—your fever? obsession? and sanity?
She has clung onto him with one scarf before: the storm.

Has Lucifer disobeyed his mistress, death, yet?
While time keeps on glancing over his shoulder, before the storm?

Once the earth—those breaths—can't be inflated in the coffin:
The eyesight faded, embers from the bitcoin, before the storm.

Have I arrived too late or too early to surrender?
Chả cá lã vọng for the disables, before the storm.

In what way the dream seethed, fading, flooding the body with infernos—
To assist burying opportunities, Hopelessness pursued before the storm.

She would refrain from weeping, she would keep kindness to herself;
She would of course, to control her heartbreaks, before the storm.

Phú Quốc has been Vietnamese to me only this century, just me—
To shake the foundation of desire before the storm.

There are munitions waiting to get on their knees for you, but are you willing?
No one can hurry the widowers, Vi, not before the storm.

Canine Lao Tzu

Watermelon seeds on the vat force me to crack
when I open them with my teeth, you stick out your tongue.

Too scorching to take a nap this afternoon nonetheless
the splintered mouths of the red seeds wink at me and I

to toss them out in the sun. They flutter like
crimson hummingbirds. The neighbors come

running by in green and yellow sandals
to witness watermelon seeds transforming

into hummingbirds near the shack where a lady
grows khổ qua and purple mangosteens. The night before

the police found a lonely shih tzu with two hundred thirty-two
fireflies trapped in the cave of his closed mouth.

When he barked a whole herd of them
rushed out of him and they fluttered in the open air

like a medium-sized passerinic city made of baby lanterns.
They flew over the rice field, the buffalos,

and zipped through áo ngũ thân on the clothesline and
above the sugarcane mills and bến xe buýt Bình Dương,

the canisters of fermented plums. Our village is a mutiny
of bò kho, French doors, dried mud after a hard rain.

As it may. Perhaps the barking dog will
wake the sleeping giant in all of us, even for

a solitary fleeing vestige. I beg that all our autumns

become like this wild thing —a village ambushed
with unexpected beauty, a landscape swarming with life,
shuddering our freedom into lanterns. Before we lose our

sandals to the monsoons, our women to the Chinese, please don't
let us forget— there is still one lantern inside of our canine Lao Tzu.

Photographs Of Photographs

To forgive the dog walker

To face reality

To chase after a lightning bolt

To recall Khashoggi's murderer

To watch the third episode of *Bodyguard* and feeling terror creeping up your back like a sniper

To beg your father to vote in the November 6th election

To remember every period stain you left on everyone else's bed

To remind your friend that you once did say, "I used to think God prefers men, but now I think men prefer men."

To dress a coffee mug in socks

To hang out with poets at a Halloween party with a doorbell clutched to your chest because you are dressed as a door and you don't want someone to ring you

To wake up from a nightmare in which a torturer debates whether to scoop your brain out with a spoon at a 5-degree angle or 10

To rejoice in inorganic blueberry muffins

To recycle a bottle of rum

To sell a pink cat blanket on eBay

To rot in a prison cell without cell phone reception

To eat canh chua cá lóc without snakehead fish in it

To drop three cubes of ice and an unripe avocado into the blender

To pull your laptop from its sleeve at the airport

To ask a Jehovah's Witness when he rings your doorbell if he would celebrate Christmas with you

To walk into Starbucks restroom without making a purchase

To surrender your smart phone at the edge of the wood

To delay the bartender from serving whiskey to the alcoholic to your left

To draw specious conclusions about Brad Pitt's future non-celebrity wife

To rendezvous momentarily with an army guard, a retarded Socialist, and watch her stomp the life out of a decapitated caterpillar as it crawls its way out of a corn taco shell

To glamorize spraying fish sauce at Donald Trump

To wonder why Fan Bingbing invites tax evasion to enter her life and to wonder if she has 883 million yuan tucked inside her bra to offset her outrageous fine

To call Pho Saigon 8 to ask if they still serve phở for breakfast for your mother

To draw a cartoon face of Richard Madden on the side of the G train

To return Leni Zumas' *Red Clocks* to the library late 23 times

To overstay one's welcome at the theatre showing porno films 24/7

To witness Michael Jackson pretending to be the illusionist Shin Lim so that Michael could bend reality not with his music but with smoking cards and impossible sleight-of-hand

To download and later delete an app that alerts you when a stranger unfriends or unfollows you from Facebook, Instragram, and Twitter

To remember the time when your sister woke up from a dream about your brother's life being in danger; and to discover that the following day that a thief, in fact, had pointed a gun at your brother while he sat in his truck at a stoplight, and he responded to the gun by pressing his foot hard down on the pedal

To take photographs of photographs with Diana Khoi Nguyen

To mourn the time when a coworker told your father to go home & he meant home as in Vietnam

To ultimately divulge that you are willing to have a wealthy husband now

To smell every single peach at a Smith's in Vegas to be certain that they are truly ripe and not to pretend that they are half-heartedly ripe

To express everything in the present tense because in Vietnamese, nothing exists in the past and nothing exists in the future, tensewise

To use, for instance, your debit and credit card at the casino until your entire retirement portfolio runs completely dry and now you can stay at least 23 days free at the MGM Grand Las Vegas Hotel and 42 free buffets for two

To take out a paint brush and paint one leaf on a tree the color of Fall and declare that Fall has already arrived in the middle of April

To drive from one state to the next until you reach a state that will let you marry your boyfriend when you are pregnant and sixteen years old

To pluck a gray hair from one's head like plucking a note from a guitar

To forget that Sunday isn't a holiday but an opportunity for overtime

After Amnesia

I wait for it to desert me.
     Even if it means succumbing to my illnesses —

as if an eyeball had fallen into a jug of water, debunking it.

At times I drink my own grave —
a soft anguish, a goodbye or a division—it has been lá cẩm
     & bird's eye chili at the hospital,

outside of my quivering.

Please don't tell me it's agony or suffering.
Allow me to follow it into an asylum.

Whatever the dictator said
     the proverb will unsay, Đi *với bụt mặc* áo *cà sa,* đi *với ma mặc* áo *giấy*—

since once the faintness of evening appears,
I find myself wearing a paper shirt, words etched in ink & written in poison.

My liver is a black market, trời ơi, distracted,
     & fierce. And if cornered to an emerald stone

I feign sadness and impossibility,
then I walk another day towards the lip of the earth—

bemused in its truncated olive blaze,

bellowing at the pasture near the edge of twilight and daybreak.
Amnesia is the same as a loaf bread—a revolt not against yeast
     against having the same uprising or memory,

an uproar baked in secular culture.

I am ambushed in the phenolic compounds—
I desire her fish basket. Her whole wrist
buried inside its eyelid.
     I don't know where I am and are you the olive branch?

after iron and selenium. I need her before the lake runs dry
Quiet now before shifting.

Slow down, as some events unfold—
     like this umbrella: upside down bánh phồng tôm.

And although you assure me that you still have a heartbeat,
I am afraid memory, once it has been encoded with olive oil,
        will say: the heart is an airport with

strict regulations on short-term or long-term
memory / parking   whatever I say—it's based entirely on
            the limbic compass

until I follow the fragrance of its demise
        the hippocampus and ngũ tạng will take over.

Tét

the north	the order	the boat
the cold	the pain	the weapon
the eye	the heart	the infantry
the hate	the refugee	the ache
the war	the defenses	the defeat
the sea	the south	the conflict
the boat	the fish	the nguyễn
the seize	the unit	the treasons
the war	the supply	the base
the force	the cost	the names
the trail	the troop	the local
the raid	the view	the rape
the bombs	the decays	the tape
the morale	the collapse	the resilience
the bury	the buried	the burying

August 22, 1960

My mother's eyes have fallen
    Asleep like
    Rice paddies
    After the monsoon season
But I woke her up
    In Vegas
    By filling her ears
    With words such as
    Madame Nhu
    Had the same birthday as you.
August 22nd
Really? She replied with half an eye open &
Fell back asleep again like a clay stone
    While the ghosts of Điện Biên Phủ
    & Ngô Đình Nhu followed
    Anthony Bourdain into a hamlet
    Salivating after the ox scent of my
    Mother's matutinal comment,
"She has a cruel face" –
Look at the way *Bà Nhu* pronounced
    "barbequed"
In English
    Anyone could tell she was cruel
    And it was her fuel for condemnation
    "Her English
Is really good!" I replied
Not in English
But in a language that sounds like saffron
    Monks lit on fire
    By a thousand hashtags
    The color of Saigon protests
    Mixed with human flesh & gasoline
Madame Nhu
    Was born on August 22, 1924
    In Hà Nội exactly
    36 years before my mother
    Offered her neonatal
    Southern breath
    Across the floral skull of Sài Gòn
    As it staged a burial flight for April 30, 1975
Trần Lệ Xuân's husband
    Was Catholic
    Like beef broth
    Is wife to anise seed, cinnamon, +
    Bone remnants

My mother doesn't fetishize cardinals or
       Deep necklines
       In áo *dài* or áo *bà ba*
We are not Việt Cộng or a bird
That's glamorous
       We are just *Việt Kiều*
       Waiting in line for our knives
       At Tân Sơn Nhất
       To cut the tongues
       Off the overripe jackfruit
       At the carousel we all donated
       Our travel fatigues to

Chở Củi Về Rừng

I am creating an app called Chở Củi Về Rừng.
Red Riding Hood cons Venmo cons Game of Thrones.
Part of the app requires that you must have already planted 500 baby pine
trees in Minnesota before you can start using it, and when you open
the app, it asks you to eat lẩu which stirs you to endorse a family of toothpicks.

To your food-embedded teeth. Don't force programmer Nguyễn
Hà Đông to design it. If he does, the flappy birds become trees
instead of columns of jade pipes with an ability to use a pistol
as well: the allegory: freedom is just a binary code away from creating
a mobile account of the The Columbine High School massacre,

where a tree becomes April 20, 1975 and tries to copycat homemade bombs,
where addiction runs rampant like a euphemistic school shooting. Block
the Coen brothers from the device. Their perversion with subversion
will make MX Player and Uber sound like Angry Birds at a Japanese market.
This app is concerning a millennial of post-Facebook users —

progenies of WeChat & deportees & groupies & outcasts — redeeming their
online coupons from corrupted promo codes. The app shouldn't have some
tacky logo inspired by an epigone of Cai Guo-Qian, the "artist who paints with
gunpowder and explosives" or Kylie Jenner. The app is not a mouthpiece for
Ariana Grande & Li Bingbing. I need Vietnamese toddlers on the school bus

with artilleries stuffed in their diapers and socks. I need glow-in-the-dark mascaras
made out of goat hair. I need Trần Thị Ngọc Ánh to bellow a short opera
whenever a user wants to exit the app. I need the app to look like a tampon or
Always maxi pads without spicy buffalo wings or an elephant sitting on a little
monkey. But this isn't an app for Asian people. This won't be an app for Asian
people. This app

won't fall off the radar because it's too complicated. This app shouldn't be
a parody for Asian people or Uber. This app won't be the voice for the Khmer
Rouge regime. This app won't be the fall of Saigon or instigate unwanted anger
amongst Việt Cộng expatriates. This app won't be the moral face of war or about
the Rwanda genocide. This app won't be about Syrian refugees. Everyone is
banned from using this app at chain

restaurants & Starbucks & Uniqlo. No right clicks on this app for Trump
supporters. No credit card purchases for student loan defaulters. & the app will
have a rape kit for women users. & no women can ever get raped when using this
app. At any rate, the only reason why I want this app to be out in the world: I just
want all women to get on the bus without being raped and to be able to use the
app while

walking alone at night, while it is still dark, while it's still dark

39

Tai vách, mạch rừng

It's impossible to grow a proverb from a river or from a lighthouse.
Over there, the wombs have been diverged. I have curated each womb
with care by resisting the procedures of the crying game. For now, all wombs
live with capital punishments. More or less, the exile of the wombs has been
forgiven by terminating each one with a clothes hanger or
a makeshift hook, thus making birthing a permissible (short-lived) protrusion.
They were caned for the Vietcong Mutiny
                    for twenty days, perhaps even
                            longer if your face looks like Agent Orange.
The Trump administration wants to know if I deem this an "Abortion poem."
In the military proverbs, I do not regard this as an herbicidal
warfare with legal consequences or a study in anthropocenic repression.

One Day I'll Have Vietnam Again

Before Đại Việt / Before Minh Mạng

Nguyễn, forget now.
The culmination of tomorrow is only a thread
& a body beneath us.
Have faith. Your water is not merely your water
till you die of thirst. As the sun undresses
its light before the mirror of the late afternoon
despite how frequently the moon
gives birth to darkness. Nguyễn,
where is your homeland? The saddest fascia
of your thought is the rings around your
memory. Another planet lives there.
Saturn, you say. And, it tells you: có công
mài sắt có ngày nên kim.
Say sorry. Then the emergency
exit glowing inside you pulsates.
There it is. Forgive. It's not like
flossing your teeth with a Band-Aid.
Near you a woman rolls down
the windshield of her heart & asks you
if you want her purse or the breeze.
When she opens the door for you in her black
linen slacks, you feel the willow tree
of your desire grow another leaflet.
how often it flutters and opens
itself before you like a second French door.
She suggests, your blouse or my house, & when you
are both alone, you touch the tips of her roofs /\
like they are the epi pen of your survival.
Even if you are not allergic to love,
please do forget: the gunpowder
is merely human ash, time fuses, pretending
to weapon-grade refugees. Nguyễn. Nguyễn,
lock your door. The saddest padlocks
are not the ones without any keyholes. & yes,
despair is when God flogs the sun
for giving out too much light. Over there
is forgiveness without resistance.
Your heartbeats falling asleep
inside you like rainwater
beneath a gutter. There, there,
your wedding ring ambushed by rice
& commitment. Love is a bowl
of ammunition & cháo lòng,
It's true, it's true— you've confused
the barrier between you and tomorrow for
bánh mì ốp la.

Once You Were Sold

Once you were sold, I stop believing in bánh bột chiên
My breath ceases suggesting tomorrow and the day after,
And sluggishly overdelivers, and begs the weak reverie of air
Your spirit had then, and of its penal unfathomable;

I worshiped your immobility with tenderness untimely or exact,
As if the price tag on your sovereignty were unconsciousable,
Clearly, a lonely freed man prized the caged mood in you,
And adored the torments of your mutable life;

And yielding beneath the aligned stars,
Susurrated, with enclosed desolation, how freedom bolted
And patrolled the lower plain of volition
While she buried her anatomy amongst a mob of bones.

Soda Xí Muội

1965

I have repaid our debt with obeisance
flogged in sweltering nước mắm.
Slash the rubicund arrow from my heart,
a thing absent created by my infancy. Melon pits skate
sadly down your knees—how bitter are you?
The amnesia of Spring hurls lurkers
near the incinerator—somehow it sulks
like tears entombed under your eyelids,
faceful of which you spasm
near my heart, near inertia.
My impartiality belongs in that hamlet,
somewhere goats could shed degenerate fur
in the inlet, excrement and urine
aching for epithelium. Are you morbid
or mendacious? The uncreased divan
is what the mountain longs for. I am no collapsing
pillow. Then I leak immortality, and soda xí muội
crawls towards us from—perhaps in an indentured rapture:
alp, potwhore, brushwood. The cyclone
inside our Catholic church fences off rabid dogs. You bend
simply to yank one grey hair out of my skull,
and use it later to floss your crooked teeth.

2018 resurgence

You threw six timecapsules
into my bơ dầm blender,
urinated a string of beads
into my fishbowl and mistook one key lime pie
for my melancholy while burning incense,
burning honey. I am afraid there
is nothing more I could say, shaking dirty rugs
from your balcony. Near the lighthouse
of Alexandria, I noticed one falcon
wore an atomic bomb vest in an attempt
to submerge a city.
An additional body surrenders
its suicidal leanings to a few disgruntled modern gods,
and below the centrifugal force of my thumb,
an army of herons sprint wildly
towards their self-immolation. Will you
ever love God more than you love me?
You convert into a water glass amid
hospital leaflets, inmate
of isolation. An ex-convict values
a pair of high heels over a cigarette

and the motion sickness of one roll of toilet paper
demands my contrition. I will only love
you tonight. Tomorrow you are my swiss army knife,
discarded and lost at sea by pure weight and blade aphasia.

The Double Doors, My Love

Until now, we'll not shame them.
Especially their nightclubs or concert halls
or their pre-Code reference to Charles Vidor
so reassuring, so reassuring.

For now, standing together they develop an impermeable theory about dual
aperture.

These vacant afternoons I've traveled over meadows, right over children and
mothers
dodging bullets to avoid some voiceover not on the radio.
I am moving along interstate 80, and have you ever been so close?
Modern windmills wave us farewell with their three arms, giant silos as big as space
shuttles,
loafing goats, hoa thiên lý, solar panels,
bruising African daises.

Beneath me, beyond me, the ground sinks, stratums of it,
the violence below đậu phụ.
Each sadness we take inside ourselves is made entirely of disappointment. Turn
around:
here is the mesosphere where cassowaries can't deepen nor empty—
unlit for months, overshadowing nights, surpassing the ambient voices
through the bellow of their sins.
Afterward, it seems that they chase the darkness
without olive oil or reflex, solely with
acute defeat.

As soon as they repose, lammergeiers sighted,
not beardlike, they don't thrash bones from great heights as we do.

As soon as we realize this — we become what?
Vultures?

The Pope believed that we are only gifted with the facility to endure torture
because
we are willing to succumb to iniquities,
but the double doors knew how to stand their ground through fitted hinges,
finding ways to create non-existent barriers between their own desire and the
outside world.
Immensity and vastness never lost faith in them.

Imagine the vacant hours with these flightless, keratinous creatures near us.
Imagine my shadow in the orchard, pulsating
soundlessly to your god in your cobalt blouse,
an indigo heavier than the sea beneath us, a cerulean murkiness shaping eagerly for

the tempests,
however heartless.

Do you know when it is a good time to commit suicide?
The final drop of light is fading
after the last leaf defoliates to exfoliate —

For the very first time in your life, won't you bring
me the razor or the blade on a silver platter
to make dying on the clawfoot tablet more effortless?

Please come near me, life—
waste no last breath on this detour.

How To Marry A Rich Man

It may not seem possible, but it has been possible: I have seduced that
Loaded man's body, his bank account, his vocal biceps
His affluent eyebrows, the way his wallet bulges in his jeans pocket
Like a second *****, but nothing tells me how to dilate his pupils

War Is Not My Mother

—after Xuân Quỳnh

How impossible it may seem. However
desperate the grenades appear to be, peace silences.
There is no breath for war. See now,
a young Việt daughter dressed in post-explosion
smiles at me with missing răng, missing fingers,
and I notice her ragged áo tứ thân, pleased
with her soft left cheek not bruised in blood.
In the aftermath, the grave helicopter twirls like a girl,
and, after offering me a handful of raw rice
garnished in grass, she disappears down the road.
And so it seems. And to forgive it all,
on this round surface alone, 815 million
children are starving
most with stomachs inflated with bags of skin
as the human shelter and broken bones as frame.
Wouldn't you want to know? How it works?: măng cầu,
unmarked graveyards, vú sữa, papayas,
Ethiopian bread, bamboo mats I bargained for mười nghìn đồng
at chợ An Đông. See what I mean. The exploding afternoon,
tactical herbicides, the gunpowder residue,
rifles stand tall like bamboo trees, trời ơi, trời ơi.
But hey, my wife is dressing a plate with ipomoea aquatica
after silencing the mouth of our broken rice
cooker with duck tapes. Your country's drones drop bombs like confetti
and near the end of our rice field is a water buffalo.
Yes, I recall: My womb is filled with ignorance. I'm war.

—*for Lâm Thị Mỹ Dạ*

Petition The Air

Asphyxiation beckons

from the outfield of desire
of vi cá, its pathetic needs.

How will you subjugate me?

Diffusing
deflection from ambulance to ambulance.

Folly spits
past sodium,

an erratic rose
windswept near your bed

You then seized
the ships of five hundred

somnolent merchants
too remote to kiss & dismiss.

The ecosphere befalls
into a dormant fetish.

Mouths for consent
and only rashly.

Mouths for sampling
mauled in an hour.

Lifetimes of submission
Split your voice in halves.

The droning and
the droning.

My misplaced
trust revisits you

like a woman with grommets
punctured throughout her flesh.

Fixated kingfishers
On the clothesline observe you

merely as stand-in windchimes
to petition the air.

After a drone appears
without supervision, I have been

forced to recoil
but the awakening

won't perish even
when I cease existing.

Freezers Who Love To Dance

We would fall asleep at night and during the nocturnal hours the freezers would wake and dance like Degas's muses into the night. Light is born and darkness isn't a man dressed in a graphite pencil or a white hoodie called an eraser. You declare that love is a snowflake that sleeps on the shoulder of a coat. Forgive me, I couldn't sedate the goddess Insomnia.

We wait for everything to saturate our mornings. Yesterday, a bird whispered into a small birdfeeder, "Don't be afraid. I am godless. Truly am." The window into anyone's soul is a bowl of uneaten snow. How to be alone when you are gone and the thermostat reads "Uống nước nhớ nguồn."

Outside the air is frantic. As if sleeping on someone's tongue is a crime even for words. Life begs you to tolerate damage while your conscience deteriorates. soon you will close your mouth with a pencil.

You left for work and there was nothing I could do to stop you from leaving me, not even hepatitis A or Medusa, to occlude and slow down the isolation, the death of sloth. When I forgive God the way you forgive, I am just a child who has eaten her own tongue and refuses to swallow ice. Won't you teach a stone to walk slowly?

I won't stop you from piling frozen tilapias into the freezers. I won't stop you from dancing with them. The lights tossing their shadows on the floor where you walk me from one side of insomnia to another. I give you my heart so you won't have to sit next to Milton, who won't cease babbling: 'What hath night to do with sleep?'

A chair's leg is warped in space. And God grows a phantom limb by making suicide possible. For all of us. We always have a quick outlet for our pain. But is it ever quick? Is it ever easy? To end a life?—to want our suffering to subside? It's true, it's true: we only want sleep, not death. We only want a second chance to wake up and be refreshed.

Sonnet Of The Consented Moan

Forever I consent you the pure spectacle
of my small bánh bèo-like mouth, or the sway
on the pale buttercup of your gasping
strokes on my breasts in the early morning.

You were fearful of existing, by that moor,
a forkless slave, and now you fret greatly
is possessing no death, chè, nor panache
for the larva of your discontent.

If I were your forbidden pearl,
if I were your god, your pre-stonewashed woe,
if you were fog, and I merely your queen,

forever I consent you the beauty you disdain,
and deck the infinite shores of my calm sea
with teardrops of my crestfallen Moaning.

To The Massacre Of Mỹ Lai

To reclaim my ephemeral visit
with Sơn Mỹ, near a sea village
in Quảng Ngãi. Wasn't it
just yesterday, you mutilate &
gang-rape your way into
March 16, 1968?
Scent of rice, unarmed children & women
ambushed by cruelty and carnage

You pretend to hallucinate:
crying toddlers as bộ đội or VC,
the outdoor morning market as
booby-traps, girls carrying
water jugs as house grenades,
And what a convenient
coverup for your baby killers,
Pinkville, pre-meditated murderers
who claimed ignorance
on chains of command

There are no repairs
for bayonets without
heads. No ammonia
or memorial or
amnesia that could rinse
away machine guns
onto mothers washing
rice in rice fields

In your most depraved
form above humid wind,
you cry, "Thảm sát là gì?"
Em ơi,
thảm sát là Mỹ Lai
You face: court-martials, fake
jail time, charges dropped,
bloodbath acquittals,
medals of honor rescinded
for your war crime.
It's a joke. It really is.

NOTES on Poetic Paintings by Numberic Words

In the summer of 2018, I taught an online poetry course. I have taught fiction before, but it was the first time I led a poetry class. In full preparation for the 10-week course, I developed a syllabus and with it the raw challenge of prompts making. Inventing prompts was an exciting pedagogical discourse for me. I get quite fanatic with it as I always try to find animated ways to get others, mainly my students, to be energetic about poetry. Before departing New York that Spring, the Clarice Lispector translator, Katrina Dodson, as a parting gift had given me a copy of Ana Cristina Cesar's *At Your Feet* that she had edited in collaboration with Brenda Hillman and her mother. While reading *At Your Feet*, I came up with an idea to get students to make their own music using words through emulation of form. Ana Cristina Cesar's poetic labor and form has been depicted as "driving recklessly" – her words just skid down the freeway of her pages with utter abandonment and blithe compulsion. Generally, I liked to test drive the prompts before giving them to my students. So we, my students and I, emulated Cesar's form by mistranslating the content of her poems. We mistranslated every single poem in *At Your Feet*. With exception to preserving some of Cesar's articles and prepositions, we substituted every single word of her poems with new ones. It was an invigorating project for everyone involved as the tangible structure of the prompt gave students and me, ironically, the freedom to create. The constraint made us quite productive and by the end of the class, I had and they too had produced an entire collection of poems borne from mistranslation. This process of mistranslation led me to figuratively notice that mistranslation was very much like paintings or coloring by numbers, except the students and I were painting with words instead. Since I saw the words through colors, I began converting the pre-conceived, preordered, and pre-generative numbers into colors. Each word Cesar uses is a number on a poetic color palette. And, instead of using the same color palettes that Cesar used to manufacture her very own poems, I invented new ones and with the invention, the birth of my own poetic transformation.

When my Cesar project ended, I shifted to employing poems by numberic words onto creating poems I discovered and read online, as online poems saved me time from having to retype the poems from scratch. I tried to imitate the forms and at times, parallel contents, of many poets as possible. The first poem I attempted with this new direction was with Traci Brimhall's famous poem, "Dear Eros" published online via VQR. I adhered strictly to her poem's structure, working vigorously not to derail as I chiseled its content to fit and embrace the linguistic, cultural, and psychological upbringing of my ontological, private self. I tried to make these paintings by numberic words as "Vietnamese" and as mine as possible. What I meant by Vietnamese is that I would try to poignantly scatter as many Vietnamese phrases, proverbs, and culinary dishes throughout. I have been told that my work was not ethic enough and what better ways to abolish this foolish observation by activately and at times "superficially" engage and incorporate my mother tongue in my work. I enjoyed the process immensely as it provided textural, syntactical, and etymological depth to my invention and gave me respite from English and a novel reason to explore the nuance of the Vietnamese language. I even learned new Vietnamese words! Words such as đậu phụ, which means tofu. I knew the word "đậu hũ" to mean tofu, but its synonym "đậu phụ" feels more poetic. What better ways to learn more Vietnamese than to write more poems in English?

While plagiarizing is frown upon in academic writing and in most commercial institutions, its distant cousin, mimicking, may seem or be viewed from afar as questionably ethical, but as I dove deep into this tricky surface, it becomes more apparent to me that my experimentation with content through form is more fundamentally Charlie Chaplin-like. In light of the Lisa Low/Claudia Cortese's devastating and polemical conflict, it may be hard to believe, but aping isn't an easy task. In fact, quite arduous. Some structures are harder to emulate than others. Danez Smith's structural "Dinosaurs in the hood" was very difficult to mimic and it took me days before I could get a hang of it. I started out matching as many white's people structures as possible and it was so thrilling converting their lyrical Caucasian impulses and conditioning into something Asian and "ethnic" and "exilic" and "exotic." What white people sound like if they were writing in Vietnamese or from an Asian mindset or upbringing or what they sound like when they were me. I also parroted poets from different eras, works by Elizabeth Bishop and William Carlos William, for examples. I started expanding the direction of my project by aping writers from different ethnic and minority backgrounds. What Iranian-Americans or Native Americans sound like if he were Vietnamese-American. How blacks reverberate if they were me and Vietnamese.

Another rhetorical device I used in the making of these poems to provoke depth of perception was to apply the antipodic method. If the original poet wrote something optimistic about an experience, I would write about it from a dark place. If Winter was mentioned, I switched the poem so it takes place in the Summer or Spring. Using negative space to create content isn't new in visual art. I had applied this technique when I drew preliminary drawings for my paintings. Intuitively speaking, it seems sensible to apply my chromatic and painterly skills into the making of poetry. There were other rhetorical devices, such as hyperbole and satire and pure mucking around, I applied to produce these poems.

It has not ceased to be obvious to me that it has been long known that editors edited anthologies of poems by others, sometimes by established or dead poets and at times by their contemporaries, as a way to celebrate and showcase their exquisite vision. Without a doubt, one thing I have done here, evidently, is subverting that traditional and making it my own self-generated anthology, ones born from Amazon suggestions, collaboration with premade or already made resources in the same fashion as Marcel Duchamp with his urinal, and universal and personal aesthetics. This is my way of crowdsourcing structures for my artistic vision. A way of making the already premade new. A way of converting and exploiting my reading consumption into tangible entities capable of being autonomous byproducts themselves. These poems may not be the hybrid cars you imagine them or be the powerful Hulk with Robert Bruce Banner inside him (Bruce Banner being the original poems, forgive my over apparent emphasis) and they may not operate efficiently as beings, but they are here and I hope you relish them as much as I like making them.

The best part about this project is to watch the original poem transitioning and transforming into different beasts in real time. Under the operating tables of my eyes and hands and keyboards, these novice poems possessing new facial compositions, mohawks and coloring, eyelashes extension, breast implants, penisic enlargement, botox on lips and hips, and with the latest post-Alexander McQueen wardrobe. In the era of trans, in the Jenner epoch, in the zeitgeist of bionics, and the ethos of self-driving solar cars, self-reliant poems like humans are no longer binary, but polyvocal, polychromatic, plural in the most adaptive sense, and unconditionally polyglottic. Not all poems here passed through the conveyor belt of plastic surgery or walked through an alienic car wash machine, to be hygienically or ontologically eviscerated, devoid of dusk and debris or bleach scoured as not to leave behind evidences of blood, saliva, human residue, or contusion. Not all poems were designed to be well-polished, or wearing fake or stick-on nails that are glued on quickly. And, for sure, no poems here are dressed like suicide bombers, exploding and creating havoc, terror, and mass destruction in their paths. In fact, quite the opposite. Some of these poems were born from a real place of hypertension, disappointment, immobility, suicide and heartaches. These poems were the ones that knew how to isolate and separate art from ennui and desire from sinew. I hope through these poems you will see fully how transient art and the making of art is. I hope you will emulate the vision and style at some point in your creative endeavors so you will realize, as I have realized, how brilliant and remarkable these original poets are in their making of these bright, fragile, potentially fugacious things called poems or paintings, if you will.

Iowa City, November 2018

Sources

Confusion
Zybum, Aline: "I Am A Lazy Bum"

Vinous Intentions
Subramaniam, Arundhathi: "Where I Live" Allied Publishers, Mumbai, 2005:
https://www.poetryinternationalweb.net/pi/site/poem/item/12083/auto/0/0/
Arundhathi-Subramaniam/WHERE-I-LIVE

Lilac & Linen
Afreen, Ishrat: "Rose & Cotton" translated by Professor C M Naim

Violets Gasping For Air
Xiuhua, Yu: "Crossing Half of China to Sleep with You" & "On the Threshing
Floor, I Chase Chickens Away" translated by Ming Di: https://www.worldlitera-
turetoday.org/2018/july/two-poems-yu-xiuhua

Northern Mourning
Qingzhao, Li: "Southern Song" translated by Wendy Chen: http://crazyhorse.
cofc.edu/featured/southern-song/

Rings Of Rebirths
Pitpreecha, Chiranan: "First Rain": https://www.festivaldepoesiademedellin.org/
en/Revista/ultimas_ediciones/71_72/pitpreecha.html

My Face In Her Dishwasher
Haengsook, Kim: "The Fall of a Face" & "Black Beach" translated from the Ko-
rean by Lei Kim: https://www.asymptotejournal.com/blog/2017/05/16/transla-
tion-tuesday-two-poems-by-kim-haengsook-2/

At Mười Giờ Rưỡi, Jesus Snapchats W/ Judas
Young-mi, Choe: "At Thirty, the Party Is Over" translated from the Korean by Sa-
rah Maguire: https://www.poetrytranslation.org/poems/at-thirty-the-party-is-over

Water & Rice
Ono no Komachi: https://www.tofugu.com/japan/ono-no-komachi/

Haiku
Yosa no Buson: "Haiku."

Sadacre
Monica Youn: "Brownacre." *The New Yorker,* May 23, 2016

Soak The Government In Ashes
Đoàn, Thị Điểm: from *Lament of the Soldier's Wife*: Foreign Languages Publishing House, Hanoi, 1966

Jacket
Hồ, Xuân Hương: "Jackfruit," translated by Marylin Chin.

You Soak & I Cry
Inés de la Cruz, Sor Juana: "Me acerco y me retiro": https://qspirit.net/sor-juana-de-la-cruz-nun-mexico/

The Church And Its Pale Betel Leaves
Anjuman, Nadia: "One Must Try," translated by Diana Arterian: https://national-translationmonth.org/wp-content/uploads/2015/12/Dark-Flower—Nadia-Anju-man-Translated-by-Diana-Arterian-NTM-2016.pdf

Hello Gothenburgers
Lorde, Audre: "A Litany for Survival" from *The Collected Poems of Audre Lorde*. W. W. Norton & Company, Inc, 2000.

Lesbian Snowflakes
Sappho: "Sapphic Fragments" translated by Julia Dubnoff: https://www.uh.edu/~cldue/texts/sappho.html

America Don't Envy Us
Holiday, Harmony: "Sex Tape or Future & Audre Lorde Fall in Love": *Poetry,* October 2017

Opium
Rich, Adrienne: "Planetarium": *The Fact of a Doorframe: Selected Poems* 1950-2001 (W. W. Norton and Company Inc., 2002)

Recklessly
Armantrout, Rae: "Advent," *Poetry,* June 2009

Orpheus Is A Verb
Girmay, Aracelis: From "The Black Maria," *Poetry*, April 2016

Within Ten Seconds
Gander, Forrest: "Abscess," from *Lynchburg*: University of Pittsburgh Press, 1993

Proverbs Of Violence
Kang, Mia: "Civitas": *Poetry,* September 2018

False Tanka(S)
Fujita, Jun: "Tanka (November)", "Tanka (A Leaf)", "Tanka (December Moon)", Tanka (Echo)": *Poetry*, June 1921

Water Bean
Elhillo, Safia: "yasmeen": *Poetry*, July/August 2018

Ectothermic Women
Lin, Joyce: "Artist Statement," January 2018: http://joyce-lin.com/artist-statement

Việt Particles War-Arranged On Sea Marine
Lê, Thị Diễm Thúy: "Shrapnel Shards on Blue Water." Ed. Lim, Shirley Goeklin. Asian-American Literature: An Anthology. Lincolnwood, Il: NTC Publishing Group, 2000.

Sổ Mũi
Trethewey, Natasha: "Miscegenation" from *Native Guard*, 2007

My Rapist Forgives My Mother For Getting In The Way Of Raping Me
Clark, Tiana: "My Therapist Wants to Know about My Relationship to Work": *Poetry Foundation*, November 2018

Dear Photograph,
Brimhall, Traci: "Dear Eros," *VQR*: Summer, 2018: https://www.vqronline.org/poetry/2018/06/dear-eros

Photograph Of The Fermented Tongue In Capsule Motel With Serrated Rasceta
Akbar, Kaveh: "Portrait of the Alcoholic Floating in Space with Severed Umbilicus," *Poetry Foundation*: Fall, 2018:
https://www.poetryfoundation.org/poetrymagazine/poems/90648/portrait-of-the-alcoholic-floating-in-space-with-severed-umbilicus

Bipartisan Monarch
Limón, Ada: "American Pharaoh," *Poets*: Winter, 2015: https://www.poets.org/poetsorg/poem/american-pharoah

Threshold
Myles, Eileen: "Holes," collected in Outlaw Bible of American Poetry, ed. Alan Kaufman. NY: *Thunder's Mouth Press*, 1999: https://jenniferstob.com/tag/eileen-myles/

Synthetic
Glück, Louise: "Vespers [In your extended absence, you permit me]," *The Ecco Press*, 1992: https://www.poets.org/poetsorg/poem/vespers

How Is It Possible That Boat People Know How To Write Poetry In English?
Abdurraqib, Hanif: "How Can Black People Write About Flowers at a Time Like This" : Originally published in Poem-a-Day on July 4, 2018, by the Academy of American Poets.
https://www.poets.org/poetsorg/poem/how-can-black-people-write-about-flowers-time

The Seven Halibut Huts
Bishop, Elizabeth: "At the Fishhouses" from *The Complete Poems, 1927-1979* © 1979, 1983 by Alice Helen Methfessel.

Before The Storm
Ali, Agha Shahid: "Even the rain": From *Call Me Ishmael Tonight* by Agha Shahid Ali.

Canine Lao Tzu
Nezhukumatathil, Aimee: "Baked Goods" from *Lucky Fish*.

Photographs Of Photographs
Sharif, Solmaz: "The Master's House": https://www.poetryfoundation.org/poetry-magazine/poems/146216/the-masters-house

After Amnesia
Diaz, Natalie: "From the Desire Field": https://www.poets.org/poetsorg/poem/desire-field

Tết
Wright, C.D.: "Flame": https://www.poetryfoundation.org/poems/51055/flame-56d22e8d6c815

August 22, 1960
Nguyễn, Hằng Nga: "August 22, 1960"

Chở Củi Về Rừng
Smith, Danez: "Dinosaurs in the hood," *Poetry*. December, 2014.
https://www.poetryfoundation.org/poetrymagazine/poems/57585/dinosaurs-in-the-hood

Soldier, Layli Long: "H̆e Sápa, One": https://www.poets.org/poetsorg/poem/he-sapa-one

One Day I'll Have Vietnam Again
Vuong, Ocean: https://www.newyorker.com/magazine/2015/05/04/someday-ill-love-ocean-vuong

Once You Were Sold
Yeats, William Butler: "When You Are Old" from *The Collected Poems of W. B. Yeats* (1989)

Soda Xí Muội
Mao, Sally Wen: "The White-Haired Girl": https://www.poetrysociety.org/psa/poetry/crossroads/own_words/Sally_Wen_Mao/

The Double Doors, My Love
Szybist, Mary: "The Troubadours Etc" from *Incarnadine*.

How To Marry A Rich Man
Hayes, Terrance: "How To Draw A Perfect Circle" *Poetry*, December 2014

War Is Not My Mother
Gay, Ross: "Sorrow Is Not My Name" from *Bringing the Shovel Down*.

Petition The Air
Bar-Nadav, Hadara: "Telephone Pole": https://therumpus.net/2013/04/national-poetry-month-day-28telephone-pole-by-hadara-bar-nadav/

Freezers Who Love To Dance
White, Allison Benis: "Frieze of Dancers," originally published in *Faultline*: http://www.allisonbeniswhite.com/frieze.html

Sonnet Of The Consented Moan
Lorca, Federico García: From *Selected Verse*, *Sonnets of Dark Love* translated by John K. Walsh and Francisco Aragon

To The Massacre Of Mỹ Lai
Williams, William Carlos: "To the Ghost of Marjorie Kinnan Rawlings," *VQR*, Autumn 1960: https://www.vqronline.org/poetry/2015/04/ghost-marjorie-kinnan-rawlings

About
Vi Khi Nao

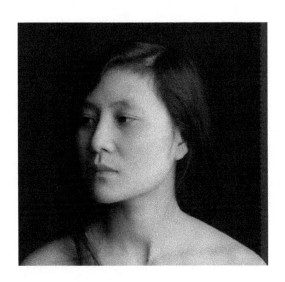

Vi Khi Nao is the author of seven poetry collections & of the short stories collection, *A Brief Alphabet of Torture* (winner of the 2016 FC2's Ronald Sukenick Innovative Fiction Prize), the novel, *Swimming with Dead Stars*. Her poetry collection, *The Old Philosopher*, won the Nightboat Books Prize for Poetry in 2014. Her book, *Suicide: the Autoimmune Disorder of the Psyche* is out of 11:11 in Spring 2023. The Fall 2019 fellow at the Black Mountain Institute, her work includes poetry, fiction, film and cross-genre collaboration. She was the 2022 recipient of the Jim Duggins, PhD Outstanding Mid-Career Novelist Prize.

vikhinao.com

ALSO BY CLASH BOOKS

SAD SEXY CATHOLIC
Lauren Milici

SEPARATION ANXIETY
Janice Lee

ALMANAC OF USELESS TALENTS
Michael Chang

INTERNET GIRLFRIEND
Stephanie Valente

THE SORROW FESTIVAL
Erin Slaughter

THE SMALLEST OF BONES
Holly Lyn Walrath

AN EXHALATION OF DEAD THINGS
Savannah Slone

LA BELLE AJAR
Adrien Ernesto Cepeda

REGRET OR SOMETHING MORE ANIMAL
Heather Bell

ARSENAL/SIN DOCUMENTOS
Francesco Levato

NAKED
Joel Amat Güell

WE PUT THE LIT IN LITERARY
clashbooks.com

 @clashbooks  @clashbooks  /clashbooks

Email
clashmediabooks@gmail.com